Bringing The Future Back – Part II

SEAN HALE

i

ISBN: 9798343954999

CONTENTS

Foreword

From Musings to Mastery - The Evolution of bringing back the future

Bringing back the future was originally conceived as a series of reflective thoughts on the intersection of technology, digital creativity, and humanity. It explored how these elements co-exist in a dynamic, ever-evolving world, and envisioned a future where they could harmoniously work together. The initial version was a collection of the author's personal musings, epiphanies, and forward-looking ideas, offering glimpses into what the future might hold.

"The original version of this book was, shall we say, a bit more philosophical - kind of like a late-night conversation with your most forward-thinking friend who insists we'll all be living on Mars in five years. While those musings were fascinating, this edition brings things back down to Earth - where the real work (and coffee breaks) happen."

But as the world continues to accelerate toward a digitally driven reality, the need for a more structured, actionable guide became evident.

Organisations today face unprecedented challenges - rapid technological advancement, shifting market conditions, and a growing need to integrate artificial intelligence (AI) into daily operations. Leaders are no longer asking "What does the future look like?" but rather, "How can we actively shape it?"

This revised edition of *bringing back the future* is a response to that question. It takes the original philosophical explorations and transforms them into a practical roadmap for navigating the future of business. Each chapter delves into key themes - innovation, digital transformation, AI integration, and emotional engagement - building upon the foundational ideas of the original work while offering concrete strategies, case studies, and actionable insights.

Each chapter is equipped with new features designed to help you move from theory to practice:

Looking Back and Moving Forward" Reflections: At the end of each chapter, you'll find reflective sections that link the original ideas with current actionable strategies. These will help you see how past ideas evolve into practical solutions for today.

Worksheet-Style Activities: To help you implement the concepts from each chapter, we've included hands-on activities that you can work on as you read the book and revisit later in your workplace. These activities are designed to guide you through real-world applications of the book's concepts, from fostering innovation to integrating AI.

Practical Case Studies and Examples: Throughout the book, you'll find generic examples that illustrate key functions and strategies that can be applied across industries. These examples are free from references to specific companies, making them applicable no matter where you work.

In many ways, this book reflects the very journey it describes. From abstract reflection to structured implementation, it mirrors the transition organisations must undergo: moving from dreaming about the future to actively building it.

"This version won't just leave you staring into space, pondering the mysteries of AI. Instead, we'll guide you step-by-step, so you can implement these ideas in your organisation and still have time to daydream about those robot butlers we were promised."

As you read, you'll notice echoes of the original concepts, but with a new layer of depth and practicality. This version is designed not just to provoke thought, but to inspire action. Whether you're a business leader, technologist, or strategist, this book offers the tools to harness the potential of the digital age, empowering you to turn vision into reality.

Welcome to the new *bringing back the future*. It's time to take the next step.

Introduction

We live in an era where the future is arriving faster than ever. Technology is evolving at an exponential rate, reshaping industries, economies, and societies. Artificial intelligence (AI) is no longer a concept relegated to sci-fi; it's integrated into everything from manufacturing to healthcare. Digital platforms are revolutionising how we work, communicate, and engage with the world. The lines between human creativity, technological capability, and business strategy are blurring.

"The future is coming at us faster than a new software update that you didn't ask for. But unlike those surprise updates, you'll actually want to know how to deal with these changes."

As we stand at this pivotal moment, it's not enough to simply react to these changes. The challenge now is to actively shape the future, to lead the transformation rather than follow it.

This book is your guide to doing just that.

"The good news? This book has your back with practical tools and strategies. The bad news? You'll actually have to use them. But hey, at least this isn't another corporate compliance training video, right?"

bringing back the future offers a roadmap for navigating the complexities of the digital age, structured around four key themes:

- **Innovation**: How can we rethink traditional business models, foster continuous innovation, and expand our capacity to generate new ideas?
- **Digital Profoundness**: How can we create deeper, more meaningful connections with our audiences in a digital-first world? How do we design experiences that resonate emotionally and build lasting engagement?
- **Dreaming Aloud**: How can businesses move beyond short-term digital fixes and embrace a long-term, continuous approach to digital transformation?
- **AI Reality**: What role will artificial intelligence play in the future of work, and how can humans and machines collaborate to unlock new potential?

In this revised edition of *bringing back the future*, we've shifted from philosophical musings about the future to a structured, practical approach that helps you implement strategies in your own organisation. We've broken down each key concept - innovation, digital transformation, emotional design, and AI - into digestible chapters with clear takeaways and actionable steps.

As you work through the book, you will encounter several new features that are designed to enhance your journey:

Looking Back and Moving Forward Reflections
At the end of each chapter, you'll find a Looking Back and Moving Forward section. These reflections connect the ideas explored in the original version of the book to their practical, updated forms in this edition. By understanding where these ideas originated and how they've evolved, you'll gain deeper insight into how to apply them in your own work. For example:

In Chapter 1 on Innovation, the Looking Back and Moving Forward section explores how the idea of "thinking outside the box" has matured into a more actionable framework for "expanding the box" through diverse teams and structured innovation processes.

In Chapter 4 on AI, you'll see how speculative discussions about AI have transformed into concrete strategies for implementing AI in a way that augments human potential and requires ethical governance.

Worksheet-Style Activities for Practical Implementation
Throughout each chapter, you'll find worksheet-style activities that allow you to apply the concepts as you go. These activities are not just theoretical exercises - they're designed to help you integrate the strategies into your daily work. Each activity focuses on specific outcomes, such as:

Chapter 2: Digital Profoundness includes an activity that guides you through designing emotional digital experiences, helping you focus on how to use storytelling and empathy to connect with your customers.

Chapter 3: Dream Aloud provides exercises for developing a digital transformation roadmap, encouraging you to think long-term about how digital tools can continuously improve your business processes.

Chapter 4: AI Reality includes a task that prompts you to evaluate which tasks in your organisation can be automated by AI and how to reskill your team for more strategic roles.

These activities can be used as real-world tools that you and your teams can return to even after finishing the book.

Real-World Examples for All Industries
In each chapter, we provide generic, industry-agnostic examples that focus on the functions and concepts, not on specific companies. These examples illustrate how organisations can implement strategies like structured innovation processes, digital transformation, and AI integration, no matter the industry. For instance:

Chapter 1 provides examples of how to create a culture of psychological safety where teams feel encouraged to share ideas without fear of failure.

Chapter 4 outlines the steps for creating an AI governance framework that ensures fairness and accountability in AI use across your organisation.

Who is This Book For?

This book is for business leaders, strategists, and innovators who understand that the future is already here - and that their success depends on how they navigate it. Whether you're a seasoned executive looking to integrate AI into your operations or a digital entrepreneur aiming to disrupt an industry, the insights in this book will equip you to lead in the next wave of transformation.

Why This Book, Now?

In today's world, change is constant, but it is no longer enough to simply keep up. The businesses that thrive will be the ones that can continuously innovate, leverage digital technologies to build deeper relationships, and collaborate with AI to unlock new efficiencies. This book is a timely guide to mastering those dynamics and turning them into competitive advantages.

What Can You Expect to Learn?

- How to build an innovation-driven culture: You'll learn how to foster a work environment that encourages creativity, experimentation, and risk-taking.
- How to design digital experiences that resonate emotionally: You'll explore the hidden depth behind digital interactions and learn how to create more profound, personalised user experiences.
- How to implement long-term digital transformation strategies: Rather than seeing digital initiatives as isolated projects, you'll learn how to approach digital transformation as an ongoing journey.
- How to harness AI to enhance, not replace, human talent: You'll gain insights into the role of AI as a collaborator in the workplace, augmenting human skills and creating new opportunities for growth.

This book is not just about predicting the future - it's about shaping it. By reading and applying the concepts here, you'll be better prepared to navigate the ever-changing business landscape and ensure your organisation is not just ready for the future, but leading it.

The future belongs to those who can dream it and then take the necessary steps to build it. Let's get started.

Innovation – Making the Box Bigger

What is Innovation Today?

Innovation is often misinterpreted as a one-time breakthrough that propels a business ahead of the competition. In reality, innovation is an ongoing process of adapting, improving, and evolving in response to changing market conditions, customer expectations, and technological advancements.

In the modern business environment, organisations must innovate not only to survive but to thrive. Given the backdrop of global competition, austerity measures, and rapidly advancing technologies, the need for innovation has never been more critical. But innovation isn't just about coming up with new ideas - it's about fostering a culture, creating systems, and building teams that can continuously generate, test, and implement those ideas.

Beyond Thinking Outside the Box: Expanding the Box

For years, we've heard the phrase, "think outside the box," suggesting that innovation requires us to abandon our current frameworks and start from scratch. But today's innovation is not about breaking out of the box - it's about expanding it. The box represents the sum of our collective experiences, skills, knowledge, and networks. The bigger the box, the more creative and practical our innovations can be.

What Does "Expanding the Box" Mean?

- **Diversity of Perspectives**: Innovation thrives on diversity. A team composed of people with varied professional backgrounds, experiences, and perspectives will inherently have a larger "box" of ideas to draw from. This diversity fuels creativity and leads to more well-rounded, inclusive solutions.
- **Leveraging Collective Knowledge**: Expanding the box means taking advantage of every resource available - be it the latest research, market insights, or lessons learned from past projects. By combining this knowledge, teams can generate more innovative and effective solutions.
- **Long-Term Thinking**: In today's fast-paced world, it's easy to fall into the trap of short-term innovation - solving immediate problems without thinking of long-term sustainability. Expanding

the box means thinking not just about how innovation can solve today's problems but how it can set the stage for future growth and resilience.

Building an Innovation-Driven Culture

Innovation isn't just about individual ideas - it's about the collective mindset of an organisation. To foster innovation, organisations must create a culture where creativity and experimentation are not only encouraged but expected.

Key Elements of an Innovation-Driven Culture

Psychological Safety: Employees need to feel comfortable proposing new ideas without fear of ridicule or punishment. Creating an environment where it's safe to take risks and make mistakes is crucial to sparking innovation.

"Psychological safety means people should feel free to share their ideas - even if their last idea involved combining drones and pizza delivery, which, let's be honest, wasn't that bad. Just imagine a world where we're all floating in cheese."

Fail Fast, Learn Faster: Failure is a natural part of the innovation process. The key is to fail quickly, learn from those failures, and iterate rapidly. The faster you can test, fail, and adapt, the faster you can innovate.

"Innovation isn't about scoring a goal on your first try. Think of it more like a game of whack-a-mole - except instead of moles, it's endless prototypes popping up. And instead of a hammer, you're using teamwork and creativity to, well, 'whack' the best idea into shape."

Collaboration and Cross-Disciplinary Teams: Innovation rarely happens in isolation. The most innovative companies bring together people from different departments - IT, marketing, finance, R&D - to collaborate on solutions. Cross-disciplinary teams bring diverse perspectives that can challenge conventional thinking and spark creative breakthroughs.

Gamification and Fun: Innovation thrives in environments where creativity is nurtured. Introducing fun, competition, or gamification techniques can make the innovation process more engaging and dynamic. Teams can brainstorm ideas in a more relaxed, creative environment, free from the pressures of daily business operations.

Transparency and Trust: Open communication builds trust within the team, allowing members to share ideas freely. Transparency about the innovation process, feedback, and decision-making helps foster a collaborative atmosphere where everyone feels their contributions are valued.

Structuring the Innovation Process

Innovation needs structure. While creativity should be nurtured, a loose, unstructured process can lead to chaos. Having a framework helps guide innovation from idea generation through to implementation. Here's a simple yet effective structure:

Ideation

The first step is generating ideas. This can be done through brainstorming sessions, design thinking workshops, or idea crowdsourcing platforms where employees can submit their thoughts. The key to successful ideation is to generate as many ideas as possible, without judgement.

- **Tools for Ideation**: Use brainstorming tools like mind maps, or platforms like IdeaScale or Spigit, to capture ideas across the organisation.
- **Crowdsourcing Ideas**: Create a platform where employees from all levels of the organisation can submit and vote on ideas. This allows for crowdsourcing innovation from a broad talent pool.

Prototyping and Testing

Once ideas have been generated, the next step is to test them quickly through prototypes or small-scale pilots. The goal of prototyping is to get early feedback, refine the idea, and determine whether it's worth pursuing further.

- **Prototyping Tools**: Use rapid prototyping methods such as wireframing, minimum viable products (MVPs), or pilot programs.

Feedback loops from early testers help refine the concept.

Scaling Innovation

Once a prototype or pilot has proven successful, the next step is scaling it across the organisation or bringing it to market. This requires careful planning and often significant investment.

- **Scaling Tools**: Use agile methodologies to roll out innovations in stages. Make sure to allocate the necessary resources, set KPIs, and continuously measure the impact of the innovation.

Measuring Innovation Success

To ensure innovation is not just a buzzword, businesses need to measure its impact. The success of an innovation initiative can be tracked using key performance indicators (KPIs) such as:

- **Time to Market**: How quickly can an idea be turned into a product or service?
- **Return on Investment (ROI)**: What financial returns have been generated from the innovation?
- **Employee Engagement**: Are employees actively contributing to the innovation process? Are their ideas being implemented?
- **Customer Impact**: How has the innovation improved customer satisfaction, loyalty, or engagement?

By setting measurable goals for innovation, companies can ensure that their efforts are delivering tangible results.

Concepts and Advice

Expanding the Innovation Box

- **Concept**: Rather than just thinking outside the box, organisations should aim to expand the box by encouraging a wider range of experiences and perspectives. This approach means drawing from diverse professional backgrounds, skills, and ideas to create more holistic and innovative solutions.
- **Advice**: Build cross-functional teams that include individuals from

different departments, such as marketing, operations, finance, and IT. This diversity allows for creative problem-solving and more expansive thinking, leading to innovations that are informed by a broader range of insights.

Creating a Culture of Psychological Safety

- **Concept**: Innovation thrives in an environment where employees feel safe to take risks and present new ideas without fear of judgement or failure.
- **Advice**: Foster psychological safety by encouraging open dialogue and celebrating learning from failure. Regularly hold team brainstorming sessions or innovation forums where employees can present new ideas and receive constructive feedback in a supportive environment.

Structured Innovation Processes

- **Concept**: While creativity is important, it must be channelled through structured processes that guide ideas from conception to implementation. Utilising frameworks like design thinking or agile methodologies helps ensure that ideas are developed systematically and efficiently.
- **Advice**: Implement a clear innovation framework where new ideas pass through phases like ideation, prototyping, and testing. Design thinking workshops and sprints can help teams rapidly iterate on ideas and refine them before committing significant resources.

Measuring and Celebrating Innovation

- **Concept**: To sustain innovation, it is crucial to measure success and recognize contributions across the organisation. Innovation metrics and recognition programs drive ongoing participation and help maintain momentum.
- **Advice**: Create a system to track innovation progress, such as an innovation scoreboard. Highlight key achievements, early successes, and lessons learned, and regularly acknowledge team efforts during internal meetings or newsletters to keep innovation at the forefront of company culture.

Case Study: Tesla and the Power of Big-Box Innovation

Tesla is a prime example of a company that has continuously expanded the box of innovation. Rather than focusing solely on car manufacturing, Tesla expanded its scope to energy storage, self-driving technology, and even space exploration through SpaceX. By creating a culture of innovation that encourages risk-taking, rapid prototyping, and long-term thinking, Tesla has disrupted multiple industries and positioned itself as a leader in both automotive and clean energy markets.

Key Lessons from Tesla:

- **Think Big**: Innovation at Tesla is driven by ambitious goals - Elon Musk's vision of reducing humanity's reliance on fossil fuels, for instance.
- **Fail Fast, Learn Fast**: Tesla isn't afraid to fail. The company has experienced multiple setbacks, from production delays to product recalls, but it uses each failure as an opportunity to improve.
- **Cross-Industry Innovation**: Tesla expanded beyond cars to energy solutions, disrupting multiple sectors. Its innovation isn't just about products - it's about rethinking entire industries.

Looking Back

In the original version of *bringing back the future*, the exploration of innovation was largely philosophical, focusing on the importance of creative thinking and the need for organisations to break free from traditional constraints. It encouraged readers to consider innovation as a mindset rather than a mere set of practices. The emphasis was on "thinking outside the box," suggesting that innovative solutions could be achieved by challenging established norms.

While this perspective was valuable, it lacked specific frameworks or strategies that organisations could implement to foster a culture of innovation. It was a call to creativity but did not provide the actionable steps needed to translate that creativity into tangible results.

Moving Forward

As we move forward into a landscape increasingly characterised by rapid technological change and market volatility, it's clear that organisations must adopt a more structured approach to innovation. Here are actionable steps to consider:

Expand the Innovation Box: Shift the focus from merely thinking outside the box to expanding the box itself. Encourage diverse perspectives by forming cross-functional teams that bring together different skills, experiences, and backgrounds. This diversity will enhance creativity and lead to more holistic solutions.

- **Action Step**: Conduct workshops that focus on team-building and brainstorming exercises, ensuring participants from various departments collaborate on innovative projects.

Create a Culture of Psychological Safety: For innovation to thrive, employees must feel safe to express their ideas and take risks without fear of negative consequences. Foster an environment where experimentation is encouraged, and failures are viewed as learning opportunities.

- **Action Step**: Implement regular "innovation forums" where employees can share ideas and experiences without judgement, reinforcing that all contributions are valued.

Establish Structured Innovation Processes: While creativity is essential, it must be paired with a structured innovation process. Implement frameworks such as design thinking or agile methodologies that guide teams through ideation, prototyping, and testing phases.

- **Action Step**: Provide training on design thinking principles and create dedicated innovation teams responsible for driving initiatives through each phase of the innovation cycle.

Measure and Celebrate Innovation: To encourage ongoing innovation, organisations must establish metrics to track success and recognize contributions. Celebrate both small wins and significant achievements to reinforce the value of innovative efforts.

- **Action Step**: Develop an "innovation scoreboard" that highlights team achievements, projects in progress, and lessons learned. Recognize innovative efforts during company meetings or events to motivate ongoing participation.

By adopting these strategies, organisations can create a robust innovation ecosystem that not only encourages creative thinking but also translates that creativity into real-world impact. Moving from a mindset of merely "thinking outside the box" to actively expanding the box empowers businesses to navigate the complexities of the digital age successfully.

Conclusion: Creating Sustainable Innovation

Innovation is not just about generating ideas - it's about fostering a culture that encourages risk-taking, collaboration, and continuous learning. By expanding the box through diverse teams, structured processes, and a willingness to experiment, businesses can build a sustainable model for innovation that drives long-term growth and resilience.

Digital Profoudness – The Emotion Behind the Screen

Introduction: The Emotional Depth of Digital Experiences

We live in a digital age where websites, apps, social media, and other digital platforms dominate how we interact, communicate, and consume information. Yet, beyond the sleek user interfaces and seamless functionalities, there is a hidden layer that often goes unnoticed - the emotional impact of these digital interactions.

"We're not talking about making your customers cry every time they visit your website - though some tech support pages might have achieved that unintentionally. Instead, we're aiming for the good kind of emotions - like the relief you feel when you finally remember your password on the first try."

The true power of digital experiences lies not in the content itself, but in how that content resonates emotionally with users. This chapter explores how businesses can unlock the emotional depth behind digital interactions, moving from transactional to profound, emotionally-driven engagements that create lasting impact.

The Role of Emotion in Digital Engagement

Why Emotion Matters in the Digital World

Emotions play a critical role in decision-making, memory retention, and brand loyalty. While much of digital content focuses on delivering information or driving transactions, it's the emotional experiences that shape how users feel about a brand and whether they remain loyal.

For businesses, tapping into the emotional aspects of digital interaction is key to building deeper connections with their audience. Consider this: the average person spends hours each day engaging with digital content - whether scrolling through social media, visiting websites, or interacting with apps. But only a small fraction of these interactions leave a lasting emotional impression.

Examples of Emotion-Driven Digital Engagement

- **Storytelling Through Digital Media**: Consider a company like Apple, which is renowned for its product launches. Their digital presentations aren't just informative - they're emotive. Through masterful storytelling, sleek design, and inspiring messaging, Apple creates an emotional connection with their audience that goes far beyond the features of the product. This emotional bond fosters loyalty, making their customers not just buyers, but advocates.

- **Charity and Social Impact Campaigns**: Digital campaigns that evoke empathy or a sense of responsibility often have a profound effect on users. A well-designed campaign by a non-profit organisation, for instance, might include powerful visuals and stories that resonate with users, inspiring them to take action, donate, or share the message.

Uncovering Profoundness in Digital Interactions

Digital Storytelling: Bringing Emotion to the Forefront

Storytelling is one of the most effective ways to create emotional connections in the digital space. It transforms otherwise transactional experiences into meaningful ones by giving users something they can relate to, empathise with, or be inspired by. Whether it's through written content, videos, or images, storytelling helps bring the human experience into the digital realm.

Telling Stories with Technology

As technology evolves, so does our ability to tell richer, more engaging stories. Consider the integration of multimedia elements - such as interactive videos, personalised messaging, or immersive augmented reality experiences. These tools not only enhance the user experience but also evoke strong emotional responses.

The Power of Empathy in User Experience (UX) Design

A key element of creating emotional digital experiences is designing with empathy. Empathy in UX design means understanding the emotional needs of users and creating experiences that align with those feelings. It's not just about usability - it's about anticipating how the user feels at every point of interaction and designing an experience that addresses those emotions.

From Websites to Emotional Ecosystems: What's Next?

Virtual Reality (VR) and Augmented Reality (AR): The Next Emotional Frontier

While traditional digital media (websites, apps, social media) provide opportunities for emotional engagement, emerging technologies like VR and AR take digital experiences to new emotional heights. These technologies create immersive environments that stimulate multiple senses, making users feel as though they are part of the experience.

Virtual Reality (VR): VR allows users to step inside a virtual world and experience emotions in a more visceral way. Imagine a travel company using VR to let users "experience" a vacation destination before booking, or a non-profit organisation using VR to show donors the impact of their contributions in real time.

"Virtual Reality is no longer just for gamers and people who want to feel like they're riding a roller coaster in their living room. It's now a real tool for engaging your customers. Bonus points if you can avoid motion sickness in the process."

Augmented Reality (AR): AR overlays digital content onto the real world, allowing users to interact with their physical environment in new ways. This can create emotional resonance by blending the familiar (the real world) with the novel (digital elements), resulting in a sense of wonder and engagement.

The Rise of Digital Empathy Tools

Looking forward, one could imagine the development of "digital empathy" tools - software that analyses user data (behaviour, sentiment analysis, tone of voice, etc.) to deliver emotionally attuned experiences in real-time. These tools could offer personalised content, messaging, and support that responds directly to a user's emotional state.

For example, a digital health app might detect when a user is feeling anxious and immediately offer calming content - whether it's meditation guidance, encouraging messages, or suggestions for self-care activities.

Creating Digital Experiences that Resonate: A Framework for Businesses

Understand Your Audience's Emotional Drivers

The first step in creating a profound digital experience is understanding what your audience cares about. What motivates them? What challenges or frustrations do they face? Use empathy mapping to understand the emotions behind their interactions with your brand.

Empathy Mapping: A tool used to visualise what users are saying, thinking, feeling, and doing when interacting with your brand. This helps you design digital experiences that address their emotional needs.

Use Storytelling to Build Emotional Connections

Create a narrative that resonates with your users on a personal level. Whether you're sharing customer stories, highlighting your brand's mission, or showcasing your impact, storytelling is a powerful way to connect emotionally.

Practical Tip: Focus on human stories that highlight real-world experiences. Customers are more likely to engage with content that reflects their own lives or aspirations.

Design with Empathy

Go beyond usability and functionality - consider the emotional state of your users at every step of the digital journey. Use intuitive design, clear messaging, and empathetic touches to make them feel understood and supported.

Leverage Emerging Technologies

Use VR, AR, and other immersive technologies to create experiences that go beyond traditional digital media. These tools can evoke strong emotional responses by making users feel as though they are part of the story or experience.

Personalise the Experience

People are more likely to engage with content that feels tailored to them. Use data and AI to offer personalised experiences that align with each user's preferences and emotional needs. This can be as simple as personalised recommendations or as complex as creating individualised journeys through your digital platforms.

Measuring Emotional Impact: How Do You Know It's Working?

While it's easy to measure things like clicks, time spent on a page, or conversion rates, measuring emotional engagement requires more nuanced tools. Here are a few ways to gauge the emotional resonance of your digital experiences:

- **Sentiment Analysis**: Use AI tools to analyse customer feedback, comments, and reviews for emotional sentiment. Are users expressing frustration, joy, excitement, or confusion? Sentiment analysis can help you track how users are feeling about your digital experiences.
- **Engagement Metrics**: High levels of engagement (such as social media shares, comments, or repeat visits) often indicate that content resonates emotionally with users.
- **Customer Feedback and Surveys**: Direct feedback from users can provide valuable insights into the emotional impact of your digital experiences. Ask questions that explore not just what users liked, but how they felt during their interaction.

Concepts and Advice

Prioritising Emotional Design

- **Concept**: In a world saturated with digital content, companies must design digital experiences that go beyond functionality to resonate emotionally with users. Emotional design fosters deeper connections with audiences and enhances user loyalty.

- **Advice**: Focus on user research to understand the emotional drivers of your target audience. Tailor the design of your digital platforms to evoke specific emotions, whether it's comfort, excitement, or empathy, by using colours, imagery, and storytelling that aligns with these feelings.

Integrating Storytelling in Digital Platforms

- **Concept**: Storytelling is a powerful tool to create emotional resonance with users. Digital experiences that incorporate narratives can humanise the brand and make interactions more memorable.
- **Advice**: Develop a content strategy that incorporates storytelling at various touch points - whether in product descriptions, user testimonials, or brand videos. Use digital platforms to tell stories about your company's mission, the impact of your services, or the journeys of your customers.

Leveraging Emerging Technologies for Deeper Engagement

- **Concept**: Technologies like virtual reality (VR) and augmented reality (AR) enable companies to create immersive, emotionally rich experiences that captivate users and make digital interactions more engaging.
- **Advice**: Explore the use of AR or VR to give customers interactive experiences that are relevant to your business. For example, a product-based company might use AR to allow users to visualise items in their home, or a service provider might use VR to immerse clients in a demonstration of their offerings.

Building Personalized Digital Experiences

- **Concept**: Personalization helps create stronger connections with users by making them feel understood and valued. Tailored experiences are more likely to evoke emotional engagement than one-size-fits-all approaches.
- **Advice**: Use data to deliver personalised experiences for users,

from recommending relevant content to customising interfaces based on user preferences. Build systems that track user interactions and dynamically adjust what is presented based on their behaviour and needs.

Looking Back

In the original version of *bringing back the future*, the focus was on the interplay between technology and humanity, highlighting how emotional connections can be lost in digital interactions. The chapter emphasised the need for storytelling and the importance of understanding the emotional motivations behind digital experiences. These reflections encouraged us to consider how technology can enrich our lives rather than detract from them.

Moving Forward

As we move forward, businesses must recognize that emotional engagement is not just a nice-to-have; it's essential for creating loyal customers. Here are key actions to take:

- **Prioritise Emotional Design**: Begin designing digital experiences that consider users' emotional states. This means conducting user research to understand how customers feel during different interactions and designing accordingly.
- **Integrate Storytelling in Marketing**: Use storytelling techniques to convey your brand's mission and values. Create narratives that resonate with your audience, showcasing the impact of your products or services on real lives.
- **Leverage Technology for Deeper Connections**: Explore emerging technologies like virtual reality (VR) and augmented reality (AR) to create immersive experiences that evoke strong emotions. Consider how these tools can be utilised to enhance customer experiences and foster deeper relationships.

By focusing on emotional profoundness, businesses can create digital experiences that not only attract customers but also forge lasting connections, turning users into advocates.

Conclusion: The Future of Digital Profoundness

As digital technology continues to evolve, businesses must move beyond transactional interactions and embrace the power of emotional engagement. By telling compelling stories, designing with empathy, and leveraging emerging technologies like VR and AR, companies can create digital experiences that resonate on a profound, human level.

The future of digital is not just about efficiency and convenience - it's about connection. And in a world where attention is scarce, creating emotional resonance is the key to standing out, building loyalty, and driving long-term success.

Dream Aloud – Reimagining the Digital Future

Introduction: The Short-Term Fix vs. Long-Term Vision

Many businesses embark on "digital transformation" journeys with a narrow, short-term focus - cutting costs, increasing efficiency, or modernising legacy systems. While these short-term wins are important, they often result in temporary fixes that fail to deliver sustainable value.

"Digital transformation is like planting a tree - you need time, patience, and occasionally some digital fertiliser (which in this case might be a strong Wi-Fi signal). You won't see results overnight, but eventually, you'll have a sturdy foundation, and possibly some very well-nourished servers."

In the rush to implement digital solutions, organisations may overlook the broader strategic opportunities that digital transformation can offer. The true potential of going digital lies not in individual projects or cost-saving measures, but in the ability to reimagine entire business models and unlock new growth opportunities. This chapter explores how businesses can move beyond the quick fix and embrace a long-term vision of continuous digital evolution.

Digital Transformation: A Continuous Journey

Moving Beyond "One-and-Done" Digital Projects

Many businesses view digital transformation as a finite project - a one-time overhaul of systems, processes, or customer interactions that, once completed, will make them more competitive. However, digital transformation is not a one-off event - it's a continuous journey of learning, adapting, and evolving in response to technological advancements and market shifts.

The Pitfall of Short-Term Thinking

A common pitfall in digital transformation efforts is the focus on short-term goals - such as reducing operational costs or optimising processes - without considering how these changes fit into a larger, long-term strategy. While short-term improvements can deliver immediate results, they often lead to diminishing returns if not tied to a broader vision.

"Remember, digital transformation isn't a one-and-done deal. It's more

like keeping up with a never-ending stream of software updates. Just when you think you've got it all figured out, bam - new version, new jargon. The good news? You're getting really good at Googling 'what does this update mean for me?'"

The Spiral of Digital Maturity

Instead of thinking of digital transformation as a downward spiral of one-off projects, imagine it as an ascending helter-skelter - a continuous upward journey where each twist and turn represents an opportunity for growth, learning, and improvement. This spiral never ends, but it gets broader and more complex as the business accumulates knowledge, skills, and technological capabilities.

Key Aspects of a Continuous Digital Journey

- **Iteration and Adaptation**: Digital transformation should be approached with an iterative mindset, constantly learning from successes and failures. This means that every project or initiative - no matter how small - should be viewed as a learning opportunity that informs future efforts.
- **Building Digital Resilience**: In a world where technologies are constantly evolving, businesses need to build resilience into their digital strategies. This means being able to adapt quickly to new tools, platforms, and customer expectations, rather than relying on a static, one-time solution.
- **Data-Driven Decision Making**: As businesses move along the digital maturity spiral, data becomes a critical asset. By continuously collecting and analysing data from digital initiatives, companies can make informed decisions, identify new opportunities, and adjust their strategies in real-time.

Reimagining Business Models for the Digital Age

Digital is Not Just a Department - It's the Business

In the early stages of digital transformation, many organisations treat "digital" as a separate function - often relegating it to a specific department, such as IT or marketing. However, true digital transformation requires an organisation-wide shift in mindset. Digital is not just a department - it's a way of doing business.

From Incremental to Disruptive Innovation

Many businesses focus on incremental digital improvements - updating legacy systems, optimising processes, or adding digital channels to their existing operations. While these improvements are necessary, they are often not enough to compete in a rapidly evolving digital landscape. The real opportunity lies in using digital transformation to disrupt traditional business models and create entirely new value propositions.

The Digital Maturity Model: Climbing the Spiral

Stages of Digital Maturity

Digital maturity is not about the number of digital tools or platforms a business uses, but about how deeply digital is embedded in its strategy, operations, and culture. Here are the key stages of digital maturity:

Initial Digitization: At this stage, businesses are focused on digitising manual processes - replacing paper-based workflows with digital tools, implementing customer-facing apps or websites, and automating basic functions.

Key Focus: Improving efficiency, reducing costs, and streamlining operations.

Operational Integration: In this stage, businesses begin to integrate their digital initiatives across different functions - connecting digital platforms with backend systems (like CRM, ERP, or supply chain) and using data to drive decision-making.

Key Focus: Enhancing cross-functional collaboration, breaking down silos, and using digital tools to gain insights.

Strategic Transformation: Businesses that reach this stage of digital maturity have fully integrated digital into their core strategy. Digital tools are not just enablers - they are essential to delivering the company's value proposition. Data is used extensively to personalise customer experiences, optimise operations, and identify new growth opportunities.

Key Focus: Creating seamless, end-to-end digital experiences, enhancing personalization, and using real-time data analytics to drive innovation.

Disruption and Innovation: At the highest level of digital maturity, businesses are using digital tools to disrupt industries and create entirely new business models. They leverage emerging technologies like AI, blockchain, and IoT to continuously innovate and stay ahead of competitors.

Key Focus: Reimagining the business, driving disruptive innovation, and continuously adapting to emerging trends and technologies.

Practical Steps to Climb the Digital Maturity Spiral

Start with a Clear Vision: Before embarking on a digital transformation journey, businesses need to have a clear vision of where they want to go. What are the long-term goals? What kind of digital capabilities do they need to build? What customer problems are they trying to solve?

Action: Create a digital roadmap that outlines both short-term and long-term objectives, with clear milestones along the way.

Build a Digital-First Culture: For digital transformation to succeed, it must be embraced by the entire organisation, not just a select few departments. Building a digital-first culture means ensuring that every employee understands how digital tools can enhance their work and the overall business.

Action: Provide ongoing training and development programs to equip employees with digital skills and foster a culture of experimentation and continuous improvement.

Invest in Emerging Technologies: As businesses climb the digital maturity spiral, they need to invest in emerging technologies that will help them innovate and stay competitive. This could include AI and machine learning, blockchain, IoT, 5G, or cloud computing.

Action: Set aside a portion of the budget for R&D and experimentation with new technologies. Encourage cross-functional teams to collaborate on pilot projects and explore how these technologies can create value.

Use Data as a Strategic Asset: Data is the backbone of digital transformation. The ability to collect, analyse, and act on data in real-time is critical to gaining a competitive edge. Companies that are data-driven are more agile, responsive, and innovative.

Action: Implement data analytics tools that allow for real-time tracking of key performance indicators (KPIs). Use data to inform decision-making, personalise customer experiences, and optimise operations.

Foster Continuous Learning and Adaptation: Digital transformation is a never-ending journey. Businesses need to build a culture of continuous learning and adaptation, where teams regularly review their performance, learn from their successes and failures, and pivot when necessary.

Action: Conduct regular digital health checks to assess where the business is on its digital maturity journey. Identify areas for improvement and adjust strategies accordingly.

The Future of Digital: Continuous Learning and Innovation

Building a Learning Organization

In a rapidly changing digital landscape, the businesses that succeed will be those that are able to learn and adapt faster than their competitors. This requires creating a learning organisation - one that embraces experimentation, encourages feedback, and fosters a culture of continuous improvement.

Innovation as a Core Business Function

Innovation is not a one-off project or a responsibility relegated to the R&D department - it must be embedded in the DNA of the business. Companies need to create formal processes for innovation, such as innovation labs, cross-functional collaboration teams, and agile project management systems that allow for rapid prototyping and iteration.

Concepts and Advice

Establishing a Long-Term Vision for Digital Transformation

- **Concept**: Digital transformation should be treated as a continuous journey, not a single project. Businesses need a long-term vision that integrates digital tools across all operations and customer interactions.
- **Advice**: Define a long-term digital transformation strategy that aligns with your broader business goals. Set clear milestones for different phases of the transformation, focusing on how digital tools will improve both operational efficiency and customer experiences over time.

Embedding Digital in Company Culture

- **Concept**: For digital transformation to succeed, it must be embedded in the organisation's culture. Every employee, from top to bottom, should understand the importance of digital tools and be empowered to use them to improve their work.
- **Advice**: Provide training and resources to ensure that all employees are comfortable using digital tools relevant to their roles. Cultivate a mindset where digital tools are seen as key enablers for achieving business goals, rather than as standalone technologies.

Implementing Continuous Learning and Adaptation

- **Concept**: Digital transformation is not static. Organisations must continuously learn and adapt as technologies evolve and new opportunities arise. A dynamic approach ensures long-term success.
- **Advice**: Build a feedback loop into your digital transformation efforts. After every project or initiative, gather insights from both employees and customers, and use this feedback to make continuous improvements. Stay agile by constantly evaluating new technologies and integrating those that align with your evolving strategy.

Taking a Data-Driven Approach to Transformation

- **Concept**: Data is a critical driver of digital transformation, enabling businesses to make informed decisions, optimise processes, and offer personalised experiences to customers.
- **Advice**: Implement data analytics tools to monitor key performance metrics and track the impact of digital initiatives. Use this data to inform your decision-making, ensuring that each stage of the transformation is aligned with measurable business outcomes.

Looking Back

The original musings in *bringing back the future* presented a somewhat idealistic view of the future, focusing on aspirations for technological advancement and the blending of digital and human elements. It encouraged readers to dream about what the future could be, yet it lacked a concrete framework for how to achieve those dreams in practice.

Moving Forward

As we transition into a future driven by digital transformation, businesses must adopt a proactive approach. Here's how to reimagine the digital future effectively:

- **Establish a Long-Term Vision**: Clearly define your organisation's long-term goals for digital transformation. What do you want to achieve, and how will digital tools help you get there? Ensure this vision is communicated across all levels of the organisation.
- **Embrace Continuous Learning**: Foster a culture of innovation where continuous learning is prioritised. Encourage employees to experiment with new technologies and processes, and provide them with resources and training to keep their skills up-to-date.
- **Iterate and Adapt**: Implement an iterative approach to digital projects. Rather than seeing digital transformation as a one-time effort, view it as an ongoing journey where each project is a

stepping stone toward a larger goal. Learn from successes and failures to continuously improve.

By embracing this proactive, long-term mindset, businesses can move beyond short-term fixes and position themselves as leaders in the digital age.

Conclusion: From Dreaming to Doing

To succeed in the digital future, businesses must move beyond short-term fixes and embrace a long-term vision of continuous learning, adaptation, and innovation. Digital transformation is not just about updating systems or processes - it's about reimagining the business itself, finding new ways to create value, and continuously evolving in response to a dynamic, ever-changing digital landscape.

The future belongs to those who dream aloud and act boldly. By climbing the spiral of digital maturity, businesses can unlock new growth opportunities, disrupt traditional industries, and create a future where digital is not just a tool - it's the way we do business.

AI Reality – Humans and CoBots

Introduction: The Rise of CoBots

As artificial intelligence (AI) becomes increasingly embedded in the workplace, the lines between human and machine labour are rapidly shifting. In this new reality, AI is not a distant sci-fi fantasy - it's a present-day disruptor transforming industries, professions, and business models.

A key aspect of this transformation is the rise of CoBots - collaborative robots designed to work alongside humans. These machines are not here to replace human workers but to augment their abilities, handle repetitive tasks, and enhance productivity. In this chapter, we explore how AI is reshaping the workforce, the evolving relationship between humans and machines, and how businesses can prepare for a future where AI plays a central role.

AI in the Workplace: A New Kind of Collaboration

What Are CoBots?

CoBots (Collaborative Robots) are intelligent machines designed to work directly with humans in the workplace. Unlike traditional industrial robots, which often operate in isolated environments, CoBots are integrated into the human workflow, performing tasks that require precision, consistency, and efficiency.

CoBots are not limited to physical tasks. In the digital world, AI-driven software bots are increasingly taking over repetitive, time-consuming processes in fields such as finance, customer service, and healthcare. These bots, often referred to as 'digital workers', perform tasks like processing invoices, managing customer queries, or even assisting doctors with diagnosis by analysing medical data.

"Contrary to what sci-fi movies have told us, AI isn't here to take over the world, just your inbox. Instead of imagining robots plotting world domination, think of them as your slightly more efficient co-workers who never take coffee breaks (or need to)."

The Human-Machine Partnership: A Symbiotic Relationship

Humans + AI = Greater Than the Sum of Their Parts

AI and automation have sparked fears of widespread job loss, but the reality is more nuanced. AI has the potential to eliminate repetitive, low-skill tasks, allowing humans to focus on roles that require creativity, emotional intelligence, and complex problem-solving. The future of work is not about humans versus machines - it's about humans and machines working together in symbiotic collaboration.

The Power of Augmentation

Rather than replacing humans, AI has the potential to augment human capabilities. By taking over tasks that require speed, precision, and consistency, AI allows humans to focus on higher-order activities such as strategy, innovation, and customer relationships. This augmentation not only improves productivity but also enhances job satisfaction, as workers are freed from mundane, repetitive tasks.

Reskilling for the AI Age

For businesses to fully capitalise on the potential of AI, they must invest in reskilling their workforce. As AI takes over certain tasks, employees will need to learn new skills to thrive in this new reality. These skills may include:

- **Technical skills**: Understanding how to work with AI systems, from operating basic software to managing more advanced automation tools.
- **Analytical skills**: Interpreting the vast amounts of data that AI generates to make informed decisions.
- **Creativity and problem-solving**: Applying human creativity to design new processes, solve complex problems, and drive innovation.
- **Emotional intelligence**: As AI handles more transactional tasks, human workers will increasingly need to bring empathy, communication, and interpersonal skills to their roles.

AI Integration Strategies for Businesses

Identify Areas for AI Augmentation

The first step in integrating AI into the workplace is identifying the tasks and processes that can benefit from automation. These are typically repetitive, time-consuming tasks that don't require much creativity or emotional intelligence. By automating these processes, businesses can free up human workers to focus on more value-added activities.

Create a Human-Centric AI Strategy

While AI has the potential to revolutionise businesses, it's essential to remember that the human element remains irreplaceable. A successful AI integration strategy should focus on using AI to enhance, rather than replace, human workers. This means designing AI systems that work in tandem with human employees, complementing their skills and improving their overall performance.

Invest in AI Training and Education

For businesses to effectively implement AI, they need to ensure that their employees understand how to work with AI systems. This requires ongoing training and education programs that equip workers with the skills they need to thrive in an AI-driven environment. Businesses should also consider creating specialised AI roles, such as data scientists, AI trainers, and automation engineers, to manage and optimise AI tools.

Ethics and Governance: The Role of Responsible AI

Ensuring AI Transparency and Fairness

As AI becomes more integrated into business processes, it's crucial to ensure that these systems operate transparently and fairly. AI algorithms can sometimes perpetuate biases or make decisions that are difficult to explain. To address these challenges, businesses must adopt a responsible AI strategy that prioritises transparency, fairness, and accountability.

Establishing Governance Frameworks

AI governance refers to the policies, procedures, and ethical guidelines that govern the development and deployment of AI technologies within an organisation. These frameworks help ensure that AI systems are used responsibly, minimising the risks associated with privacy violations, data misuse, and biassed decision-making.

AI and Data Privacy

AI systems rely heavily on data to function, often using personal information to make decisions or generate insights. This raises important questions about privacy and data security. Businesses must ensure that they have robust data governance frameworks in place to protect sensitive information and comply with data protection regulations like GDPR.

The Future of Work: CoBots in Every Industry

Manufacturing and Robotics

The manufacturing industry is one of the earliest adopters of CoBots, with robots performing repetitive tasks such as welding, painting, and assembly. As AI technology advances, CoBots are becoming more sophisticated, capable of performing more complex tasks and adapting to new environments.

Healthcare and AI-Driven Diagnostics

In healthcare, AI systems are being used to analyse medical data, identify patterns, and assist doctors with diagnosis. AI-powered tools can process vast amounts of medical information in real-time, helping doctors make more accurate and timely decisions.

Retail and Personalization

Retailers are using AI to create personalised shopping experiences for their customers. From AI-driven chatbots that provide personalised recommendations to automated warehouses that process orders faster, AI is transforming the retail industry by enhancing efficiency and improving customer satisfaction.

Preparing for the AI Future: What Businesses Can Do Today

Adopt an AI-First Mindset: Businesses should start viewing AI not as a distant technology, but as a critical part of their strategic toolkit. This means actively looking for areas where AI can add value and integrating it into long-term business plans.

Create a Culture of Continuous Learning: As AI technology evolves, so too must the workforce. Encourage a culture of lifelong learning by providing employees with access to AI training programs, workshops, and resources.

Prioritise Ethical AI: Ensure that your AI systems are designed and deployed ethically. This includes addressing potential biases in algorithms, ensuring transparency in decision-making, and complying with data privacy regulations.

Foster Human-AI Collaboration: Rather than fearing job displacement, focus on how AI can complement human workers. Invest in tools that allow for seamless human-AI collaboration, such as AI-powered assistants, chatbots, and data analytics tools that enhance decision-making.

Concepts and Advice

Promoting AI as an Augmentative Tool

- **Concept**: AI should be seen as a tool to augment human capabilities, not as a replacement for human workers. By automating repetitive tasks, AI allows employees to focus on higher-value, strategic work.
- **Advice**: Identify processes within your business that are repetitive and can be automated using AI. These might include data entry, scheduling, or routine customer interactions. This will free up human talent to concentrate on creativity, problem-solving, and decision-making.

Investing in Workforce Reskilling

- **Concept**: As AI takes over certain job functions, businesses must reskill their workforce to ensure employees can work alongside AI effectively. This includes both technical skills for AI management and soft skills like creativity and emotional intelligence.
- **Advice**: Develop training programs that teach employees how to interact with AI tools, while also focusing on developing critical thinking, innovation, and interpersonal skills. Create opportunities for employees to apply their newly acquired skills in collaboration with AI-driven technologies.

Establishing Ethical AI Governance

- **Concept**: Implementing AI at scale requires careful attention to ethics and governance. Ensuring that AI systems operate transparently, fairly, and without bias is crucial to maintaining trust and accountability.
- **Advice**: Establish governance frameworks that oversee the use of AI in your organisation. These frameworks should include policies for data privacy, algorithmic transparency, and the mitigation of biases. Regular audits of AI systems should be conducted to ensure compliance with ethical standards.

Creating Human-AI Collaboration Strategies

- **Concept**: Effective AI integration requires collaboration between humans and AI systems. Both should complement each other, with AI handling tasks suited to machines and humans focusing on creativity, empathy, and leadership.
- **Advice**: Design workflows where AI supports human roles rather than replaces them. For example, use AI for data analysis and pattern recognition, while humans interpret the results and make strategic decisions. Ensure that your AI systems are designed to be intuitive and enhance human performance.

Looking Back

In the original version, discussions around AI were more speculative, exploring futuristic scenarios where humans and machines would coexist. It highlighted concerns about AI taking over jobs but lacked a deeper examination of how AI could enhance human capabilities in the workplace.

Moving Forward

As AI becomes an integral part of our work environment, businesses must focus on fostering a collaborative relationship between humans and AI. Here's how to move forward effectively:

Promote AI as an Augmentative Tool: Position AI as a collaborator that enhances human performance rather than a competitor. Educate employees on how AI can take over repetitive tasks, allowing them to focus on higher-value activities that require creativity and emotional intelligence.

Invest in Reskilling Programs: Develop comprehensive reskilling initiatives to prepare your workforce for an AI-driven environment. Offer training programs that focus on both technical skills (e.g., data analysis, machine learning) and soft skills (e.g., creativity, critical thinking) to ensure employees can thrive alongside AI.

Establish Ethical AI Governance: As AI systems are deployed, it is essential to implement governance frameworks that address ethical considerations. This includes ensuring transparency, fairness, and accountability in AI decision-making processes. Create a cross-functional committee to oversee AI initiatives and address any ethical concerns.

By fostering a collaborative and ethical approach to AI integration, businesses can harness the full potential of these technologies while empowering their workforce to thrive in the evolving landscape.

Conclusion: Humans, AI, and the Future of Work

The rise of AI and CoBots is transforming the way we work, but the future is not about machines taking over - it's about creating a harmonious partnership between humans and AI. By embracing AI as a tool for augmentation, reskilling the workforce, and prioritising ethical governance, businesses can thrive in an AI-driven future.

The key to success in this new reality is adaptability. As AI continues to evolve, so too must our approaches to work, learning, and collaboration. Those businesses that embrace AI and harness its potential will not only stay competitive - they will lead the way in shaping the future of work.

From Vision to Action

As we reach the end of this journey, it's time to reflect on the path we've taken through *bringing back the future*. What began as a series of forward-thinking musings has transformed into a practical guide for navigating the complexities of today's digital and technological landscape. We have explored the power of innovation, the emotional depth behind digital experiences, the continuous nature of digital transformation, and the role of AI in shaping the future of work. Now, as we close this chapter, it's important to shift focus to the most critical part of the journey: action.

In a world where technology is evolving at breakneck speed, where customer expectations are higher than ever, and where AI is transforming industries, it's not enough to simply understand these concepts. The true challenge is in applying them - leading your organisation, your team, or yourself through the next phase of growth and transformation.

"By now, you've tackled innovation, emotional design, digital transformation, and AI. You're basically a time-travelling business guru, ready to take on the future - one automated process and digital interaction at a time. Or at the very least, you've learned how not to panic every time someone says 'machine learning.'"

This final chapter summarises the key lessons from each stage of the book and offers a call to action: to take what you've learned and begin implementing it today. The future won't wait, and those who act decisively now will be the ones who shape it.

A Recap of the Journey

Chapter 1: Innovation - Making the Box Bigger

We started by reframing innovation. It's no longer just about thinking outside the box - it's about expanding the box. The most innovative organisations bring together diverse teams, encourage psychological safety, and implement structured processes to take creative ideas from concept to reality. Innovation thrives when failure is seen as a stepping stone to success, and when employees are empowered to experiment and take risks.

Chapter 2: Digital Profoundness - The Emotion Behind the Screen

In the digital age, it's not just about having a presence online - it's about creating meaningful, emotionally resonant experiences. We explored how businesses can use storytelling, design with empathy, and leverage emerging technologies like AR and VR to connect with their customers on a deeper level. The future of digital is about moving beyond transactions and building lasting, emotional relationships with audiences.

Chapter 3: Dream Aloud - Reimagining the Digital Future

Digital transformation is not a one-time event - it's a continuous journey. We discussed how businesses must move beyond short-term digital fixes and embrace a long-term vision of iterative learning, adaptation, and innovation. Digital maturity is not about having the latest technology; it's about how deeply digital is embedded in your culture, strategy, and daily operations.

Chapter 4: AI Reality - Humans and CoBots

AI is here, but its role is not to replace humans - it's to augment human potential. We explored how AI can take over repetitive tasks, allowing human workers to focus on higher-value activities like creativity, problem-solving, and strategic thinking. The key to thriving in an AI-driven future is reskilling the workforce, fostering human-AI collaboration, and establishing ethical governance to ensure AI is used responsibly.

Looking Ahead: The Call to Action

The concepts explored in this book are not just theoretical - they are the building blocks of the future. The key question is: **What will you do next?**

The time for reflection is over. It's time to take action. Here's how you can start implementing what you've learned:

1. Start Expanding Your Innovation Box Today

Innovation begins with fostering a culture that encourages creativity, collaboration, and risk-taking. Start by assembling diverse teams, introducing structured innovation processes, and providing psychological safety for employees to share their ideas. Encourage experimentation, and don't fear failure - use it as a tool for learning and improvement.

Action Step: Launch an internal innovation lab or platform where employees can propose ideas, collaborate across departments, and pilot new projects.

2. Build Emotional Depth Into Your Digital Experiences

As you refine your digital strategy, focus on creating experiences that go beyond functionality. Design with empathy, tell stories that resonate emotionally with your audience, and explore new technologies like VR and AR to create immersive, engaging experiences.

Action Step: Audit your digital touchpoints - website, social media, apps - and identify opportunities to introduce more meaningful, emotional storytelling.

3. Commit to Long-Term Digital Transformation

Digital transformation is not something that can be completed in a quarter or a fiscal year - it's an ongoing process. Start by evaluating your current digital maturity and creating a roadmap for continuous improvement. Integrate digital into every aspect of your business, from customer interactions to internal processes, and foster a culture of learning and adaptation.

Action Step: Create a digital transformation task force to oversee the implementation of digital initiatives, track progress, and ensure that digital maturity remains a top priority.

4. Leverage AI to Augment Your Workforce

AI is a powerful tool, but its success depends on how it's integrated into your organisation. Start by identifying areas where AI can automate low-value tasks, freeing up your human employees for more strategic roles. Invest in reskilling programs to ensure your workforce is equipped to collaborate with AI effectively.

Action Step: Conduct an AI readiness assessment to identify areas where automation and AI could be integrated into your processes, then create a plan for gradual AI implementation and workforce reskilling.

The Future Belongs to the Bold

The future is coming at us faster than ever. The businesses that thrive will not be those that merely react to change but those that anticipate it and actively shape it. The concepts in this book are not just ideas - they are strategies for survival and success in the modern world. By embracing innovation, deepening your digital connections, committing to continuous transformation, and collaborating with AI, you position yourself and your organisation to lead in the next era of business.

Now is the time to act. The future won't wait, and neither should you.

So, how will you bring the future back to your organisation? What will you do to lead, innovate, and thrive in the digital age?

"The future isn't going to shape itself, unless you've got a self-shaping future tool (and if so, please share it with the rest of us). It's time to roll up your sleeves and put all this new knowledge to work. And if things go sideways? Well, at least you've got this book as your guide. We promise it won't self-destruct."

This is your call to action. Take the first step today and start shaping the future.

Activities

Activity 1: Expanding the Innovation Box

Objective: Encourage diverse, cross-functional collaboration to enhance creative problem-solving.

Task:

- Identify a challenge or problem your organisation is facing.
- Form a team of 5–7 people from different departments (e.g., marketing, operations, IT, finance, customer service).
- Hold a brainstorming session where each team member contributes solutions based on their unique expertise.
- Use a mind map to connect these ideas and look for patterns or innovative combinations that emerge from the discussion.
- Afterward, summarise the session by identifying the top three actionable ideas.

Reflection: How did diversity in perspectives influence the range of ideas generated? Were there any surprising connections between departments?

Activity 2: Creating a Culture of Psychological Safety

Objective: Build an environment where employees feel safe to express ideas and take risks.

Task:

- Host a 30-minute "Innovation Forum" where team members can propose ideas without judgement.
- Set clear guidelines: there are no bad ideas, and every suggestion will receive constructive feedback.
- Track the participation rate - are team members freely contributing? What kind of ideas are being shared?
- At the end, vote on the most promising idea and create an action

plan for testing it.

Reflection: Did team members seem hesitant or open to sharing their ideas? What steps can you take to improve psychological safety in future sessions?

Activity 3: Structured Innovation Processes

Objective: Implement a structured approach to innovation to move from ideation to implementation.

Task:

- Choose an innovation framework (e.g., design thinking, agile methodology) and outline its steps (e.g., ideation, prototyping, testing).
- Identify a small project or problem that can serve as a pilot for using this framework.
- Lead the team through each phase of the framework, ensuring that all participants understand the process and their role.
- Track progress, hold brief check-in meetings, and document learnings at each step.

Reflection: How did the structured process help guide your team? Were there any challenges in keeping the team aligned with the process?

Activity 4: Measuring and Celebrating Innovation

Objective: Create a system to track innovation success and celebrate contributions.

Task:

Develop an "Innovation Scoreboard" for your team or department. Include columns for:

- Idea
- Project lead
- Current phase (ideation, testing, etc.)
- Impact (potential or realised)

- Review the scoreboard weekly to discuss progress and challenges.
- At the end of the month, hold a meeting to celebrate small wins and showcase any successful projects.

Reflection: How did the scoreboard help in keeping the team focused and motivated? Did celebrating wins increase team engagement?

Chapter 2: Digital Profoundness - The Emotion Behind the Screen

Activity 1: Prioritising Emotional Design

Objective: Design digital experiences that resonate emotionally with your audience.

Task:

- Review a key digital touchpoint in your organisation (e.g., your website homepage, mobile app, or product page).
- Identify three emotional triggers you want users to feel when interacting with that touchpoint (e.g., excitement, comfort, trust).
- Make a list of design elements (e.g., colours, imagery, language) that could evoke those emotions.
- Redesign a section of your digital platform with these emotional triggers in mind and test it with a sample group of users.

Reflection: What emotional reactions did the users have? Did the design elements achieve the desired emotional effect?

Activity 2: Integrating Storytelling in Digital Platforms

Objective: Use storytelling to create emotional connections with users across digital platforms.

Task:

- Select a product or service you want to promote.
- Develop a brief, 3-part narrative structure (Problem, Solution, Transformation) that shows how your product or service impacts the customer's life.
- Apply this story across different digital touchpoints: website,

social media, email marketing.

- Track user engagement (clicks, shares, comments) to see how the story resonates with your audience.

Reflection: How did users respond to the storytelling approach? What insights did you gain about the emotional connection your audience has with your brand?

Activity 3: Leveraging Emerging Technologies for Deeper Engagement

Objective: Explore the use of VR, AR, or other emerging technologies to create immersive digital experiences.

Task:

- Identify a product, service, or experience in your business that could benefit from immersive technology.
- Research the available tools or platforms (e.g., AR apps, 360-degree video) that can help create an interactive experience.
- Design a basic prototype of this immersive experience and test it with a small group of users.
- Collect feedback on how the users felt during the experience and what emotions it evoked.

Reflection: How did the immersive experience impact user engagement? What technical or emotional challenges arose in creating the experience?

Activity 4: Building Personalized Digital Experiences

Objective: Create personalised user experiences by leveraging data and insights.

Task:

- Audit your current digital user journey. Identify areas where personalization could be applied (e.g., recommendations, tailored content).
- Implement simple personalization strategies, such as segmenting email campaigns or offering personalised product suggestions.

- Track how personalization affects engagement metrics (click-through rates, time spent on site, etc.).

Reflection: What impact did personalization have on user behaviour? Did personalised content create a stronger connection with your users?

Chapter 3: Dream Aloud - Reimagining the Digital Future

Activity 1: Establishing a Long-Term Vision for Digital Transformation

Objective: Define a long-term vision and strategy for your organisation's digital transformation journey.

Task:

- Hold a strategic meeting with key stakeholders to discuss your company's long-term digital transformation goals.
- Use a digital transformation roadmap template to outline key milestones over the next 1, 3, and 5 years.
- Identify the digital tools, systems, and processes that need to be integrated or improved to meet these goals.
- Assign responsibilities for each phase of the roadmap and schedule periodic reviews to assess progress.

Reflection: How clear is your organisation's vision for digital transformation? Are the milestones realistic and aligned with your broader business objectives?

Activity 2: Embedding Digital in Company Culture

Objective: Foster a culture where digital tools and practices are integral to everyday operations.

Task:

- Organise a company-wide workshop or training series focused on digital literacy and tools.
- Introduce a system where employees can propose digital solutions to improve workflows, customer service, or internal communications.
- Create a reward or recognition program for employees who successfully implement digital tools that enhance efficiency or user experience.

Reflection: How has the use of digital tools improved work processes? Are employees more comfortable with digital practices, and are they embracing them in their daily tasks?

Activity 3: Implementing Continuous Learning and Adaptation

Objective: Build continuous learning and adaptation into your digital transformation approach.

Task:

- Conduct a "lessons learned" review after each digital initiative or project. Document key insights, challenges, and successes.
- Use the feedback to adjust future digital projects, ensuring that your team is constantly improving based on past experiences.
- Create an internal knowledge-sharing platform where employees can access and contribute insights on digital tools and technologies.

Reflection: How well is your team adapting to new technologies and feedback? Are lessons from past projects improving the success of new initiatives?

Chapter 4: AI Reality - Humans and CoBots

Activity 1: Promoting AI as an Augmentative Tool

Objective: Identify areas where AI can augment human capabilities in your organisation.

Task:

- Review current business processes and identify repetitive, low-value tasks that can be automated.
- Research AI tools that could automate these tasks (e.g., data entry, scheduling, customer service queries).
- Implement an AI solution and track how much time is saved and how human roles can shift toward more strategic activities.

Reflection: How has the introduction of AI changed the nature of work for your team? Are employees able to focus more on higher-value tasks?

Activity 2: Investing in Workforce Reskilling

Objective: Develop a reskilling program to prepare employees for AI-driven roles.

Task:

- Conduct a skills gap analysis to determine which employees need reskilling in areas like data analysis, AI tool management, or creativity.
- Design and deliver training workshops or courses that focus on both technical AI skills and soft skills (e.g., problem-solving, emotional intelligence).
- Monitor employees' progress and offer opportunities for them to apply their new skills in AI-enabled roles.

Reflection: How well are employees adapting to their new skills? Has the reskilling effort improved collaboration between AI tools and human workers?

Activity 3: Establishing Ethical AI Governance

Objective: Implement ethical governance frameworks for AI use.

Task:

- Draft an AI governance policy that outlines ethical guidelines for AI use, including transparency, fairness, and privacy.
- Form a cross-functional committee to oversee AI deployment and ensure compliance with ethical standards.
- Conduct regular audits of AI systems to check for biases or ethical concerns and adjust the systems accordingly.

Reflection: How effective is your AI governance framework in maintaining ethical standards? Are there areas where AI bias or transparency need improvement?

www.ingramcontent.com/pod-product-compliance
Lightning Source LLC
Chambersburg PA
CBHW040231240726
48664CB00001B/90